Brown Bag Brigadier

Gary John Miller

Made with ❤ on the BookLeaf Publishing Platform
www.bookleafpub.in
www.bookleafpub.com

Dedication

Dedicated to Austin & Troy,

The funniest brothers I could ever hope for.

Preface

This book is the result of a 21-day challenge I set for myself—to write and publish a poem every single day. Each poem in this collection was crafted with the intent to capture a fleeting moment or a persistent feeling, born from the daily rhythm of life—chaotic, reflective, and sometimes messy. What began as an experiment to challenge myself quickly turned into an unexpected adventure, full of surprises, discoveries, and moments of pure joy. Each poem reflects not just my thoughts, but a deeper exploration into different forms, styles, and techniques—sometimes fluid, other times rigid, but always with the goal of pushing my boundaries as a writer. The idea was simple: to experiment, to have fun, and to see what I could create in just three weeks. I wanted to dive into different poetic forms, stretch my creative muscles, and challenge myself to step out of my comfort zone. Some days it felt easy, other days it was a grind, but in the end, it all came together. And what emerged was more than just a collection of poems—it became a time capsule, a snapshot of where I was at that moment.

this collection is a reflection of my journey, my challenges, and my joy in discovering new ways to express the thoughts swirling around in my mind. And, just as importantly, it's an invitation for you to challenge yourself too—to explore, to create, and to have fun in the process.

Enjoy the ride, and thank you for being part of it.

Gary John Miller

Acknowledgements

This book wouldn't exist without the people who inspire me, encourage me, and remind me why words matter.

To my wife, Suzanne—your love and support fuel everything I do. Thank you for always believing in me, even when I'm lost in a sea of scribbles. You are my rock, my confidant, and my biggest cheerleader.

To the writers I've admired—your words have shaped the way I see language, rhythm, and the magic of a well-placed line. This book is a small tribute to the art you've created. Your work continues to challenge and inspire me every day.

To my brothers—You are my rocks, the people I want to be a good example for. Your friendship, humor, and loyalty mean the world to me, and I'm endlessly grateful to have you by my side.

And to my parents—you are the true spirit of *The Cold Lunch Brigadier.* Tough and gentle, always willing to help others in need and very often unseen. The daily struggle lived. Thank you for filling my world with stories, laughter, and the kind of encouragement that makes anything feel possible. You've taught me the value of perseverance, kindness, and the importance of living authentically.

To Professor Rebecca Wee, whose guidance in poetry at Augustana College helped shape my voice and deepened my love for the craft.

To all my professors who have challenged me, pushed me, and helped me grow as a writer.

To **BookLeaf Publishing** for giving me the opportunity to bring this collection to life and for believing in this project.

To my followers on social media and all the supporters who cheered me on throughout this journey—your encouragement means the world.

And to the vast wealth of poetry resources available today. It's never been easier to find new forms, techniques, and inspiration to try. Thank you to everyone who continues to keep poetry alive and accessible.

To all of you, thank you for being the foundation on which this work was built

1. Daydreaming in a Dilapidated House

The tongue tousled teeth,
outmuscled in wit—
dentures dent the demon's grip.

A word whistled through,
midst a gapped-tooth grin—
cheese to eat and cheese to smile.

Each joke, like a tick,
wiggles in his ears—
laughter shakes the spine of time.

Money hums on screens,
memory distorts—
TV flickers fever-pitched.

Half-past any clock,
ticking bites the skin—
lice have made a home in me.

Bed bugs think I bite back,
sleeping through the day—
night unravels, dark and long.

Kites fly me to France,
queen of ants dine cheese—
knees too straight for them to dance.

Falling Apart, scaffolds stitched
ghosts of families and the haunting
echoes of laugh tracks

2. Bubblegum Moon

I unwrapped a card,
wishing for the gum—
but the king had banned the chew.

Blowing bubbles bold,
grandma grinned and puffed—
gums on gums, she grew and grew.

One day, up she went,
floating through the sky—
sticking pink across the moon.

They say long ago,
cheese was in its place—
now it's made of taffy glue.

The man on the moon
blew a wad so big,
gum fell down into the sea.

Tigers try to chew,
but their teeth protest—
gorillas are best at this.

Chests of hairy mess,
sticky strands of pink—
chew and chew, then blew and blew.

Big lungs full of air,
inhale, swell, expand—
I will float to Everest.

Past pyramids,
and ancient stone walls,
see the sun rise in the Nile.
Wave to a grinning crododile.

I'll climb the Great Wall,
and taste the Taj Mahal,
floating 'til I see them all.

3. Poem About The Poem

Across the written forms; the soul is starved &
Raging for sustenance. We flay falsehood, shedding
Spiritual masks—solipsistic echoes of the universe,

Parabolas spiraling from a funnel of the word,
One utterance beyond heaven or hell,
Echo into echo, clicks & clacks of desperate
transmission.
Time bargains with us, and we concede in ink,
Inking human stains on letters without addresses,
Conversing with ghosts of past, present, and future.
And yet, we call it a silly poem—crumple it, and chase
Sysyphus.

4. Bedtime For Bansai

The child's world spun and swirled,
He jumped, twirled, no fear of splats,
Pretend cats, then a monster—
A lobster, circus acrobats.

The creature leaps up higher,
A flyer tired of the ground,
Unlocks his wild dreadlocks—
Tarzan walks the trees unbound.

Careful not to make a sound,
Mom's ears hound for waking boys.
Sleep is her prized possession,
Use discretion, no ape noise.

Finally, after hours of jumping,
This thumping little gorilla,
Saws logs and counts dancing sheep,
No peep to stir awake Momzilla.

5. Miracles on Parade

A Miracle claimer made a calm reclaim
On Elder crime relics.
Empires reaped, raped, and raided
Malice came and made a deep ideal
Married a laced idea.
Cradle clamped and marred.
Admire a real dream came, a leader.
Miracles on parade repaired, reclaimed, replaced.
A primal creed dreams. A Leader, a limper.
A lame limp leader leads.
A dear pearl parades a miracle, a reclaimer.

6. Be. Becoming. I evolve. I am more. Transforming into everything I was meant to be.

Am

Am

Am I

I am a waste.

I am breathing, still . . .

. . . But I am wasted potential.

Stirred by impulse, I seize the pen and write my way out of the box.

In and out, breathing words like water and fire—ease.

All I had to do was act. Move.

Vibrate in motion.

Move oceans.

Live life.

Be.

Becoming.

7. Nestling

Blue soft baby bird bellowed,
First worms swallowed,
Momma's angels,
Safe from danger.

Perched high in a church gable,
Flying unable,
To leave the nest—
Digest and rest.

Mom tells stories of leaving home,
Touch the blue dome,
Heaven, the sky—
One day I'll fly.

8. Kintsugi Toro Bravo

I was a bull in a China shop
I admired the beautiful
Decorations, as they crashed –
I was not made for ballet
But a deadly tango.
We breathe our last.
Artists in red.
You and me –
Mi amor
0
Charge.
Fight me.
Adorno,
My end is yours.
Cornada por ti –
Empiezo a bailar
Danza de la muerte.
Aquí, mi razón de ser.
Porcelain shatters, veins of gold bleed.

9. The Jim Brown Ouroboros

A Mouse trap caught me while I was buying a burger from a clown.

He had sharp red edges around his mouth, the same
type of corners I was caught in when I threw up two fists
and told you to bring armageddon upon me.
I love nothing more than fighting out of a corner.
King of the beef.
Unrivaled and wearing high heels on a high horse
taking the bridge under the high road.
I fight dirty like a pugilistic pig-pen in a prize fight
punching Peanut Tillman.
Clack my pretty pink heels together to get halfway
home.
Queen of the plains.
I have a wicked mind, green with jealousy at your
famous little rants.
We all listen with waxed ears.
Queen, King, Pawn, we're all the same at dawn.
Call me Dorothy.
I make friends like I'm going home, and I'll never forget
you.

Lions, Tigers, and Bears.

I've never met any, but I've smoked a couple camels,
drank shots of sterno, and picked out popcorn kernels
from the teeth of fire-breathing dragons.
I've pumped up crowds like Adidas shoes, fell in love
easier than dolphins on acid being studied by NASA.
Kinetic like a Connecticut cold cut, nonsensical like a
polished pillow popsicle corpuscle.
At this moment, I looked into the mirror and it all made
sense.

Reflect upon yourself. Learn from yourself.

There are more sides than the other half of you.
At the moment, I heard myself speak to myself to myself
to myself.

"Anna Grammer renarg Anna."

Instructing myself to speak clearly.
I asked for the name.

"Anna, Bob, Hannah, Otto."

I thought about Jim Otto. He wore two zeros. Played for
the Raiders.
Symmetry is so goofy.

11. 22. 33. 44. 55. 66. 77. 88. 99.
The last one. The Great one. Gretzky.
I am 32. The Jim Brown year. Next year I'll be 33.

33 AD. The beginning of time as we know it., As we
measure it. What system did the dinosaurs measure it in?

Could they?

Of course they couldn't.

But what if they could.

It was a breakthrough and divine opening of the third
eye.
The other two squinted, too. tired and red.

 I saw a shiny halo above my head.

A rattlesnake ouroboros.

 "In girum imus nocte et consumimur igni."

 Virgil, how clever.
Rows and rows of doors behind. Opened and shut at the
same time.
 My mind gnashed, was it a rat I saw?

"Go dog Go,"

How patronizing.

I heard a sound.

They heard a sound.

Echo. Echo. Echo.

The same but different. Same, same but different. Same
the same.

Tattarrattat. Tattarrattat. Tattarrattat. Tattarrattat.

I thought of childhood rituals.
I'm afraid of the calling out to darkness. The part of this
heart is the artist and the hardest part is that it's marred
charred and scarred in need of a kickstart and it goes
from a muscle to a sweetheart.
I don't want to invite it in.
We would stand in front of the mirror and see fear in
our eyes as we called out to Mary.
Whoever she was, she never seemed to come.
Perhaps she was forgiving.
She could see in our hearts we didn't want to invite her.

It's not polite to show up bloody and a mess.
We'd stay up late playing games.
Halo. That was often the one.
Master Chief had no fear, nor would I.
What about the other games?
The one with the Race Car Level?

"Madam, in Eden, I'm Adam."

So, we begin.
 What was the first thought Adam had when he saw
Eve?
What year? When did we begin?
**Carbon dating seems like a terrible way to meet a
woman.**
 I imagine he couldn't keep his eyes off of her.
 She was the first of her kind.
 An improvement over man.
 I look at myself in the mirror and I admire everything
God improved on.
 I love me, but I don't like to look at me.
 Women, they are so much prettier than me.
First there was darkness, a rich blanket of silence and
deep thought.
 It must have felt like finding the right words to say.
 Then a second of time goes by and a whisper followed
by the light, divided by thirds, the seen, the unseen, and

the unknown.

I imagine the sky and waters came fourth, rushing like sentences out of a child with questions at a circus.

The water must have loved the feel of the moon.

The moon is peaceful that way.

It wanes and pulls.

That could have been five days in?

Was that when the land anchored the sea?

Perhaps it was the 6th day on which the moon kisses the sun and stars.

She's so giving in her affection.

I look down at the clock.

Tomorrow comes early.

I'm more tired now than I was at the beginning.

I had a lot of fight in me.

I could fight out of corners.

I could survive off seven-up and eschew 8 hours of sleep.

"I wish I was 9 years old again."

Just to play Halo with my friends one more time.

The ouroboros above me reminds me that time is a flat circle.

Something I watched McConaughey say in *True Detective.*

I didn't understand it until I saw him in *Interstellar* and I

realized memory and love are ways we time travel.
Forward and back. Across time and space.
Life is conical and comical.
In comedy we call it routine.
The comedian has to keep us on our toes.
Make me listen.

"I've heard this joke before"

But I forget the punchline.
Can't help but laugh. I forgot how funny it was.
Cosmic comedy.
The only club we're dying to get in.
A dad joke inserted into a thought piece. Glossed over by
a serious brown highlighting answers for the test put
forth by the almighty that was never given in the first
place.
A test of a test of a test.

It doesn't matter how old I am, I'm always here.
I'm always there.
 I have always been elsewhere.
 I will grow young and die old.
 I will talk softly and whisper loudly.
 Living in a paradox like Gary John Connor Miller.
I exist in the sacred and the profane.

It's like finding wisdom in a beer ad tagline.
There is no time.
Time is an illusion.
The only time, is party time.

Never odd or even.

10. The Water Cycle

I have an interview coming up.
I need my emotional support water bottle

I am leaving my country to live in another.
I need my emotional support water bottle

I miss my brothers.
I miss my parents.
I miss my nieces and nephews.
I need my emotional support water bottle

I miss the dinner performances and the
mispronunciations of adult words.
They used to say bisgusting instead of disgusting.
Nuggle instead of snuggle.
We say it more than they do.
I need my emotional support water bottle

I am learning to speak another language.
I say hello and thank you with so much energy.
It's all I know how to say and I want it to say more.
I need my emotional support water bottle

I am a fish out of water.
I am a fish in friendly waters.
They are teaching me to swim differently.
I am flowing.
I need my emotional support water bottle

I must be like water.
As Bruce Lee once said.
I see snow is man-made here in Thailand.
I need my emotional support water bottle

Paradise can't have everything.
I need my emotional support water bottle

I am home wherever my heart is.
I am a nomad, wandering.
I am like the water.
Visiting, desiring to leave things better than I found it
and to move on.
I want to see the world.
One drop at a time.

11. Cold Lunch Trading Post

Cold Lunch, Bold Munch, Old Hunch, Sold a Bunch.
Pop Tarts, peanut butter, praying packed potato pringles.
The brigade trades in mom's notes.
Famous Last Words.
I did not get my Spaghetti-O's;
I got spaghetti.
I want the press to know.

12. Sestina For Adventurous Boys

We carried lit torches and wick lanterns,
 Explored stalagmite caves, where echoes
 Bounced off walls, our secrets spilling—
 As if each secret were a thread
 In our kinship. We shared hunger,
 Splitting a stolen bologna sandwich from the frozen
vault.

The fridge—we called it a vault.
 The flashlight was my lantern.
 We had eaten dinner, but we still hungered
 For adventure and wonder, hearing our names in the
echoes—
 Dreaming of sailing past the needle-thread
 Of Scylla and Charybdis, past oil spills.

My friend whispered a secret. I told him, "Spill."
 A first crush felt raw, like a tiger freed from a vault.
 A smile poked through a thin thread
 Of smoke, his grin caught in the lantern's
 Glow. He whispered again, too softly. I asked, and the
echoes
 Carried it back—he liked the girl with the pink bow. Oh,

hunger.

A heart always hungers
 For more than we can put into words. We feared spilling
—

 Afraid to break like glass, our voices mere echoes.
 We locked up dreams like treasure in a vault,
 Buried in heart-shaped caves, the lanterns
 Dimly flickering, as if burning a single thread.

Young friendship wove tight like the fates' thread.
 We watched over each other—no one went hungry
 If the other did. If I fell, you'd raise a lantern,
 Pouring from your cup into mine, spilling
 Love freely, leaving none in the vault.
 The stalagmites rose like cathedrals, and prayers became
echoes.

Those before us had left their echoes,
 Their voices still carried in an unseen thread.
 We stood on their shoulders, dreaming of vaults
 Of pirate gold and hidden wonders, our hunger
 For discovery unquenched. We stole beers and spilled
 Dad's frozen stash—warmth flickered under lanterns.
 The cave was our vault, where boyhood wonder echoed.
 We raised our lanterns to darkness, unraveling threads
 Of fear. Our hungry hearts spilled joy into each other's.

13. ハンバーガーとおもちや (Hamburger & Toy)

The Lion King toy,
McDonald's Happy Meal joy,
A blonde little boy.

Recycled meal box,
Tricking the boy into eating—
Mom's home-cooked real meals.

Cheap toy ploys for kids,
Fast food playpens, energy,
Burned from cheeseburgers.

A place to play free,
Birthday kids celebrating,
With cake and cheap toys.

Perspective says this:
Every meal is a happy meal.

14. Bad Guys on Television

Bounty Hunting as an occupation.
We made plans in the 2nd grade to meet,
We even had a city, state, and a street.
Dreams seeded from games on our Playstation.
Boba Fett's known deadly reputation,
Bebop's Spike Spiegel was in our heartbeat,
Boys with guns dancing in their heads, ready to
Point at the bad guy association.

Wanted to be a cowboy that day,
The towers fell, and a villain appeared.
A TV screen, a window to dreams, smoke cleared,
We marched into war, I wanted to play.
Innocence longs for a yesterday,
Cowboy shootouts, Jedi Wars, acne feared,
"Be all that you can be," just don't be gay.

Marine, a football player, surely,
These were in my future as a grown man,
Colored me in crayon drawings, a plan.
It's achievable, meant to be for me.
A doctor at one point I wanted to be.
My dexterity, fumbling hand,
Military dreams, maybe a Frogman?

I don't swim well, think more maturely.

Was Clint Eastwood paid well for his service?
Was it worth a fistful of dollar bills?
Or was it worth a few dollars more still?
Asking if there are good guys who hurt us.
There were more ways to make evil nervous,
Justice was the objective, let's be real.
Bad guys and bullets, that's life in a reel.
The job is meant to serve you, not serve us.

15. The Father's March

The step must be forward,
 Head in the light direction,
 With honor and your word.

Burn ships and march toward
 The shoreward. No misdirection.
 Unsheath your sword.

Wild men fighting the horde,
 Mortal men, not waiting for a chosen one,
 The step must be forward.

From the day you cut the umbilical cord,
 Until you come home on shield to warm reception,
 When spirit is restored.

The day on which we meet the Lord,
 I never turned to salt through deception,
 The step must be forward.

I knew what I was marching toward,
 Caring not for my perception,
 The step must be forward.

16. Around Here

Meter maid, minute made,
 Fire hydrant, water park,
 Kids sold ice-cold lemonade.
 Here is where I stayed.

Coming home in the dark,
 Time stood still when we played,
 Living life like an exclamation mark.

Times I wouldn't trade,
 Like hot dogs at the ballpark,
 Napping under an oak tree's shade—
 Here is where I stayed.

17. King Edward Lives For a Day

King Edward perched on his porch swing,
 Grew saddled with anxiety, never using his wings.
 He measured his life in more losses than wins,
 Always felt left out, never quite in.

He rocked back and forth on his porch until he greyed,
 Thought of the lighthouse, the wharf's eye swayed.
Fear of deep waters, what lies beneath when he's adrift.
 Sharp sharks with harpoon marks, his mind starts to drift.
 The hubris of Atlantis buried beneath the rift.
 he dreams as he hold's water, black stars in the light sky
—the mighty *If.*

Lost at sea, he hears the thunder.
 It keeps him guided, from falling under.
 The water turns from blue to red.

The ocean's depths to the universe a puddle.
 Zeus's bolts and Thor's hammer duel.
 Pay the gods what they are due.
 For they see life as but a story.

Mighty cyclops' eyes defiled,
Poseidon heard his name as he fled.
Nobody can do anything, the odyssey he led.
If not nobody, you can call me Ed.

Ed built a boat with the wood from a soapbox,
 Challenging giants like Jack with his beanstalk.
He'd steal fire like Prometheus,
 in a soapbox ship fit for Theseus.

Oh! mighty Ed, to an island far away,
 Sails with oars from hardware stores,
 Frolics in wordplay,
 And sails to distant shores.

18. If The Map Doesn't Agree With The Ground, The Map Is Wrong

We ignore the evidence in front of us,
 see the smoking gun and still light a cigarette from the barrel,
 inhaling carcinogens that numb the sharp edges of living.
Every generation hears, "*don't do drugs*"
We might as well hear it with ear plugs.

We've done this for years—
we know life's hard.
We feel it, live it,
and still bring babies into the world.

We give them tooth fairies dealing in cold currency,
 slipping coins under pillows where she pilfers teeth.
Where do they go? What's the trade?
I imagine they must be sustenance,
like milk for growing bodies.
I saw milk ads in the classroom,
 white mustaches asking if I had any.
Juiced-up baseball players chugging dairy,

while I wondered why I couldn't hit home runs.
Wrestlers told me to eat my vitamins,
to say my prayers—when they didn't live theirs.
It's easy to get cynical.

The world sucks,
and when we figure that out, we stay there.
We read the map, look at the ground,
see the cracks, and ask questions—
but the mapmaker insists:
The map is right. Keep digging.
Shape the ground to fit the map.
But life isn't tucked in Dora's backpack,
laid out in three simple steps.
The ground needs footsteps,
the wind's music, the plants speaking.
Go wild. Learn to listen.
Follow the stars. The compass points north.
Find landmarks. Find your way.
If the ground and the map don't get along—
trust your gut.
Truth isn't buried, bought, or drawn.
It's found in fragments,
held in your hands,
pieced together like a mosaic of meaning.

Truth needs a voice.

One day, you realize life doesn't suck
  the way you first thought when you grew up.
  Wisdom isn't about growing up at all—
  it's knowing that pretending to be an adult is pointless.
The tooth fairy was never about the money—
  it was a way for our parents to say they loved us,
  to make us believe in adventure,
  that magic was real.
Sure, baseball players weren't really drinking milk,
  and the dairy industry was selling a dream,
  but hey—chocolate milk was damn good,
  and a little extra calcium never hurt.

We bargain with our brains,
make peace with with what was sold and what was real.

We heard more preaching than acting,
  but we were meant to learn by seeing.

Every generation builds,
  plants seeds for the future.

The world isn't darkness and vampires,
  emo music and black velvet Elvis.
  But it's not sunshine and rainbows either—
  Lisa Frank notebooks and talking dolphins.

It's somewhere in between—
like a dollar slice of pizza
in the middle of Hell's Kitchen
burning the roof of your mouth but still worth every
bite.

19. I am the Denverine

I carry a homemade meal everywhere I go.
 Pack a lunch, bring a bunch—
 that's what I heard them say.
Calloused hands swing hammers,
 ten-ton slammer, ham-and-egger,
 giving generous grace.

Brown Bag Brigadier, open the
brown bag facing friend.
Share a lunch, bring a bunch.
Playground rhymes punching
cap'n crunch, be a friend
in order to be befriended.
Sit with me, I
 have room at my table, always.

Bucking Bronco busy bustling.
Wrestling words into works.

Get a grip, get real they told me.
You're out of touch.

These hands have held twisting tornadoes,
 riding the romantic rodeo.

branded a bronze bull belt buckles
 bragging you better bring it, I'm brave and ready
for a brawl.
Circled cyclones
hurried hurricanes, moved mountains
mashed mustard seeds onto
Chicago dogs with a midwestern
politeness and work ethic, A door
opening Rodeo-roping, rope-a-doping,
 can of cope open, grinning with a dip in.
Rizzle ripping rub the chalk grip in.

Brown Bag with sour snacks, snack packs
sandwich bags, and a can of can do.

Persistently optimistic like sally on the seashore
selling things you can get for free.

Location, location, location.

A simple man, no happiness found
 in a rich man's gold.

Home sweet home—under the stars, I roam,
 roping rawhides, wrestling,
 running like a rascal.

The cascades of Casper, a Cheyenne beach,
 I've seen the great white buffalo
 hail from Spirit Lake.
 I won the West,
 quick-draw hands with six shots each.

Fists of fury and palms of peace,
 a contradiction confidently feeling the right amount of
guilt.

I am the Denverine.

I've seen a blanket of snow
 stretch across Colorado,
 frozen lakes where my ancestors hunted.

Western hands have held a cyclone in the East,
 putting it to sleep
 with a lullaby and a cowboy song,
 gentle and sweet.

The earth is an inheritance
 for the lowly and meek,
 simple treasures—these are what I seek.

The wind will talk and carry my fame—
 we were a cyclone before he came.

The Broncos busting Brown Bag Brigadier,
at least, I think that was his name.

20. Dictionary Gary

I began to think, why do they call it "sprinkle"? **Wrinkle.**
A silly word—who came up with Pterodactyl?
Zygodactyl?
What the hell does that even mean? **Zygotene**?
I have a date with a dictionary. **Gary.**

Searching for words to describe how I feel at this stage of
life.

Cracking, cackling, crackling forward, backing,
 Tackling, sacking, math ain't mathing, laughing,
subtracting
 Tracking, packing, slapping, lasting, wrapping—
 A game of life, crashing, smashing, no laughing,
stage players acting, no capping, still snappy snapping,
What's happening? Half-ling happy tapping tactfully
taffy
bootstrapping – onwards and upwards.

Fashioning passion. Cashin compassionate
Action, like Samuel L. Jackson,

 camera smash in.

Blast it, I read right past it.

21. 1 Mile More

As unsung heroes sing along to their own song,
 Even if they don't know the words, they sing it loudly.
First in, last out.
 Must win, no doubt.
 In the thick of it,
 Think thin thoughts,
 Unconcerned with clout.
Melting, smeltering, pelting welts—
 Like punishment dealt from belts, yelping.
 Bring the heat if it's hot, like inviting white lightning
indoors, frightening.
 Do the right thing, fight in the ring.
Ding, ding.
King took a right hook swing and exited the left wing.
Ding, ding.
Say anything—
 Nothing, one thing, something.
Why do you make it so hard on yourself?
 "Hey, boss, I like chaos to find out what I'm about."
Helter-skelter, the shelter's felt the weight,
 The welter of worries, then a pause, a wait.
 No time to waste—shimmer bright, no dimmer,
 The dark night here, but you keep getting brighter.
 Nightlights in twilight, bright sights light,

Bring on the daylight, alright, alright, alright.
Climber of no mountain higher,
Like Wim Hof in the winter, you're chasing fire,
Pinned a sinner, reverse Uno for the winner.
Run of the litter, never been a quitter,
Truth spitter, fibber hitter, no bullshitter.
If I'm being honest, a damn good babysitter.
Cracking, cackling, with life's laughable grace,
In the fire, comfortable at my own pace.
Out-mazing rats like it's a turtle race,
Amazing cats like it's an easy hurdle to face.